THE MURDER OF ANNA MARIA

The True Story of William Burgess and the Wheal Eliza Mine.

Gail Crane

Published by Aller Books

website: https://gailcranewriter.com

Front Cover Image: The Grave of Anna Maria Burgess
© 2023 Barry Hitchcox
Back Cover Image: by kind permission of The Exmoor Society.

Paperback: ISBN: 978-1-73997 16-9-4
Ebook: ISBN: 978-1-73997 16-8-7

CONTENTS

INTRODUCTION

In 1858, in the isolated village of Simonsbath on Exmoor, the death of a six-year-old child by her father's hand shocked the small community.

The story of Anna Maria Burgess and the Wheal Eliza mine has since taken its place among the myths and legends of Exmoor.

The story has been told many times and, as with any story that has been told and retold as this one has been over the years, there are conflicting accounts and differences of opinion. So what really happened? What is the true version?

With the help of parish records, newspaper archives, contemporary reports of the murder and of the trial, and Ancestry.com, I have tried to piece together an accurate picture of the events that led to the deaths of Anna Maria and of William Burgess.

There are still gaps, and it is not possible to verify all reports. Newspapers then, as now, were selective with the facts and each reporter put his own spin on the story.

When a story fires the imagination as this one did, there will always be errors and inconsistencies, so it is doubtful the whole truth of the matter will ever be known; but it is my hope that this account might come close to it.

MAP OF THE AREA

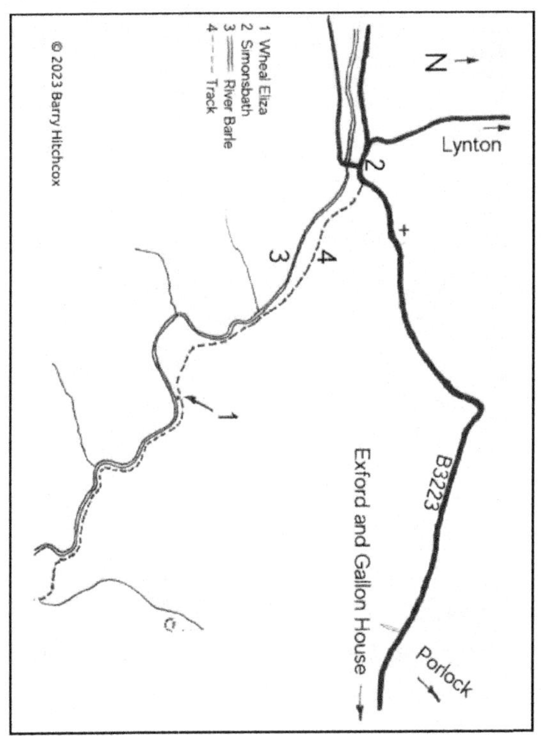

WILLIAM BURGESS

William Burgess was born around 1816, in the village of Porlock on Exmoor. He was the son of John Burgess, a mariner from Bossington, and his wife, Betty Floyd. John and Betty had three other children; a daughter, Betty, and two sons; an elder son John, and a second son who was said to have died in a lunatic asylum.

As a teenager, William Burgess worked as an agricultural labourer, tending the stock that roamed the Exmoor Forest. Even at that early age, one of his employers warned him that, if he didn't learn to control his temper and aggressive behaviour, he was likely to end his days on the gallows.

Burgess could neither read nor write and was seen by all who knew him as a wastrel and a drunkard; a regular visitor to the taverns of South Molton.

The Bridgwater Mercury, reporting on his trial in January 1859, gives a detailed description of him.

His appearance was that of a rough, hard-working labourer, and his countenance, when in repose, though far from prepossessing, indicated only a rugged coarseness incidental to his position in life. He was described as 43 years of age, but might have been taken for a few years older. His complexion was fair, eyes blue, face rather broad, and the distance from the nose to the bottom of the chin rather short. His height was about 5 feet 10 or 11 inches; his frame apparently powerful, though it did not seem muscular.

The Wells Journal, on 15th January 1859, noted that: *he was deplorably ignorant.*

He must have had some redeeming features, however, for, in 1838, he courted and won Jane Shapland, daughter of George Shapland, an Excise man from Exford. The banns were called in St Dubricius church in Porlock, and on 28th October 1838, William Burgess and Jane Shapland were married in the church of St Mary Magdelene in Exford.

They set up home in Slate Quarry Cottage in White Water Combe, about a mile east of the Wheal Eliza mine, and not far from the slate quarry and iron mine that existed nearby at Picked Stones.

During the nineteen years of their marriage, Jane gave birth to five children: Mary born 1840, Jane born 1844, John born 1846, Charles born 1849, and Hannah Maria born 1852.

In most present-day accounts of the story, Hannah is referred to as 'Anna' but in contemporary accounts, in the newspapers of the day, she is invariably called Hannah.

For a while, all went reasonably well. Burgess continued to work as an agricultural labourer, and marriage to Jane seemed to have a steadying influence on him.

Then, for some unknown reason, he decided they were all going to emigrate to America and, with that in mind, he sold what few goods they had and left for Bristol, where he intended to find a berth on an emigrant ship.

The plan was that, when he reached America, he would send for his wife and children. But it was not to be. He actually did make it as far as Bristol but, instead of taking ship to America as arranged, he went, instead, to Wales, where he proceeded to embark on a drinking spree which resulted in him losing almost all the money he had taken with him.

Almost penniless, he now had no choice but to go home. He returned to Exmoor, where he managed to recover some of the goods he had sold, and resumed life with his long-suffering wife and family.

All this took a heavy toll on Jane. Never of strong constitution, and no doubt worn down by the trials of life with Burgess, Jane became ill. She caught measles and developed an inflammation of the lungs and, on 7th February 1857, she died. Shortly afterwards, she was buried at St Andrew's church in Withypool.

Burgess's reputation was well-known and rumours

quickly spread throughout the community that he had killed her, but the nurse, Rebecca Barwell, and the doctor, Mr Spicer from North Molton, who had both attended Jane, certified that her death was from natural causes.

To add to Burgess's troubles, around that same time, his youngest son, Charles, had the misfortune to break his thigh. The cost of medical treatment for his son, added to the costs of Jane's illness and death, left Burgess struggling to find enough money to live on.

Lacking the steadying influence of his wife, he quickly reverted to his old ways, visiting the taverns, and spending any money he did manage to scrape together, on drink. Rarely sober, and becoming increasingly belligerent, he eventually lost his job.

He now had no employment and no money, and he had five children to support.

Unable to find work, Burgess was not too proud to resort to begging and approached the parish vicar, Reverend William Thornton, for help. Initially, Thornton was completely taken in by Burgess's sorry tale of his plight and, thanks to Thornton's efforts, the villagers took pity on Burgess and rallied round to help.

A sum of money was raised to help him support the children but, far from using it for the benefit of his family, Burgess spent it all on alcohol. As a result, he completely lost the goodwill of Thornton and of the villagers, who refused to have anything more to do with him.

Unable to support the children, and desperate to find some means of getting them off his hands, Burgess decided to try and place them in service at local farms. His wife, Jane, had relatives on Exmoor; farming families who, he thought, would surely have need of extra help and might, therefore, take the children in.

One of Jane's sisters, Mary Shapland, had married John Hayes at Porlock in 1827, and they were now farming at Brinsworthy near High Bullen in Devon. John and Mary agreed to take two of the children; Jane, now 15 years old, to work as a dairymaid, and Charles, now 10 years old, to work as a cow boy.

Burgess did his best to persuade them to take Anna as well but, although they initially agreed, for some reason, possibly because Mary was expecting another child, they later changed their minds and the arrangement was called off.

Mary's husband, John Hayes, had a brother, James. In 1855, James had married Sarah Dascombe and taken her to live at Southhill Farm at Withypool, the home of his parents, John and Mary Hayes. In that same year, shortly after his marriage, James's mother, Mary, died and James took over most of the running of the farm.

Also living at Southhill, were Matthew Shapland and Grace Shapland, possibly cousins or other relatives of Jane's.

When Burgess approached him, James agreed to

take the two older children, Mary now aged 16, and John now aged 12, as servants, but he would not take Anna, saying he already had enough people to look after. Burgess pleaded with him, but James was adamant.

Furious at James's refusal, Burgess left the house in a blind rage and, possibly under the influence of drink, and completely regardless of the fact that his own children were in the house, he took revenge by setting light to the farmhouse.

In the fire that followed, John Hayes, Matthew Shapland, and Grace Shapland all lost their lives.

As Burgess was not arrested at the time, it is probable there were no witnesses and no evidence.

Anna, at only six years old, was too young to be put into service, but Burgess eventually managed to find her a home with the local blacksmith, John Steer, who lived with his wife Agness and family at Exford Cottage in Exford. Here, by all accounts, Anna was well looked after and happy, and the family grew fond of her.

Then, in 1858, Burgess took her away from the Steers. The reason is not known, but it was almost certainly just so he could save the two shillings a week he was paying for her keep and use it, instead, to support his drinking habit.

He had now moved into lodgings at Gallon House Cottage, the home of John and Sarah Marley.

The cottage, on what is now the B3323 between

Exford and Simonsbath, stood on the opposite side of the road to the Gallon House Inn, sometimes known as the Red Deer Inn. It was part of Red Deer Farm which had been purchased by Frederick Knight in 1841, and where Knight held his biannual rent audit for the Exmoor and Brendon Estates.

While here, according to Mrs Marley's evidence at the trial, and that of fellow miner, William Cockram, Burgess was employed at the Picked Stones iron mine, on the White Water. His work entailed removing the waste rock and other materials that had been dug out of the mine; a job known as *'taking off the deads'*.

On 26th June 1858, he took Anna to live with him at the Marley's. Why he did this is not clear. It was a highly unsatisfactory arrangement as she was obliged to share a room, and a bed, with him and his fellow lodger, William Cockram. It could not have been on account of the cost, as the Steers had charged him 2s for her keep whereas Mrs Marley charged him 2s 6d a week.

Was the move the first stage of his plan for Anna?

In return for the extra rent, Mrs Marley looked after Anna, fed her, and did her washing. Burgess was earning 2s a day at the mine, so 2s 6d a week for Anna's keep does not sound unmanageable. It seems Anna was happy at the cottage, playing with the Marley's children and being well cared for by Mrs Marley.

Then, just a month after bringing Anna to live

with him, on 24th July 1858, Burgess informed Mrs Marley he was taking her to live with his mother at Porlock, and asked her to get her ready and pack some clothes for her.

He left his lodgings early one morning taking Anna with him. He returned later that same day; alone.

A member of the household remarked that *'he was returned very early considering the distance to Porlock and back was some fourteen miles'*. The inference seems clear. Had he really been to Porlock as he claimed?

That thought must have been in people's minds when, a couple of weeks later, on 10th August, Burgess informed everyone he had decided to move to Porlock himself, in order to search for work.

He left Simonsbath that same day; and disappeared. He never arrived in Porlock.

Again, the villagers began to wonder about Anna. Where was she? Might something have happened to her, too?

Reverend Thornton, having been taken in by Burgess once, and being well aware of his dubious character, was also suspicious. He sent the Forrester, William Court, to Porlock to see Burgess's mother, but told him not to say anything to her about Anna being missing.

Court returned, saying he had seen Mrs Burgess and she had confirmed that Burgess had been to see her on the Sunday as he had told everyone, but that he had been alone and she hadn't seen him since. Court said he had seen no sign of Anna in the village.

Burgess's brother-in-law, John Moore, speaking at Burgess's trial in 1859, said Burgess had approached him to take Anna in, but that '*she had never come*', and Burgess had never mentioned it again.

On the morning of 17th August, John Mills was walking across the fields behind the Gallon House, on his way to work on his father's farm, when he noticed the remains of a fire on one of the allotments.

Curious, he went to investigate. Wondering what it was that had been burnt there, he stirred the heap with a stick and found in the ashes some pieces of cotton fabric, some fur, and some buttons and hooks and eyes.

Mary Farley, who lived next door to the Marley's, also went to the allotment to have a look, and found amongst the burnt clothing a piece of Anna's pinafore.

She took the pieces to Mrs Marley who recognised them as the clothes she had packed for Anna to take with her when she left with her father. Afraid for what it might mean, she took them to Police Constable George Taylor, who immediately contacted Police Superintendent Cresant Jeffs at Wiveliscombe.

Some accounts say that Thornton then undertook a five hour ride from Simonsbath to Curry Rivel, a distance of 45 miles, in order to consult Valentine

Goold, the Chief Constable of Somerset, who then returned with him. There is no mention of this anywhere in contemporary accounts and it does beg the question, why, on a matter of such urgency, would he make such a long journey when Superintendent Jeffs was at Wiveliscombe police station only 24 miles away?

Together, Jeffs and Taylor searched the area and examined the ashes, where they found other remnants of clothing which were identified as belonging to Anna.

A search was immediately set in motion and, about a mile across the moor from the Gallon House Inn, and not far from where the fire had been lit, some mine workers found what appeared to be a recently dug grave. It was along the valley near the Wheal Eliza mine and Picked Stones where Burgess had been employed just prior to his disappearance.

At first it was thought just to be a hiding place for a stolen sheep. Sheep theft was common and thieves would often bury the carcass in a shallow grave as a temporary measure, coming back to retrieve it later when it was safe to do so. However, when Jeffs examined it, he noted there was a strong odour of decomposing animal matter and, on closer examination, found signs that a body had recently been buried there for a short time before being moved elsewhere.

The discovery of the grave, combined with Burgess's sudden disappearance, convinced Jeffs that Anna had indeed been murdered, and he immediately published a handbill offering a reward of £10 for anyone discovering her body.

Word quickly spread round the village *that Anna's father had done her in.*

Fearing Burgess might try to get away by sea to Wales before he could be apprehended, Jeffs rode to Lynmouth, but he was too late to stop him. On arrival at the fishing port, he discovered Burgess had already escaped, having crossed by fishing boat to Swansea.

Jeffs followed him to Wales, where he found him working as a navvy at the new docks then being constructed at Swansea. He arrested him and searched his lodgings where, amongst his belongings, he found a pair of child's boots which he suspected were Anna's, though Burgess protested they were a pair he'd had made for one of his boys.

They returned to Simonsbath, where Burgess was questioned by Thornton, who pleaded with him to say what he had done with Anna, but Burgess refused to say anything.

When Sarah Marley saw the boots Jeffs had found in Burgess's Swansea lodgings, she identified them as the ones Anna had been wearing when they left Gallon House Cottage.

This was all the evidence Jeffs needed. Burgess was taken to gaol in Dulverton, where he was brought before magistrates, M Bissett, J A Locke and Captain Bernard. After hearing evidence from witnesses,

Burgess was told he would be committed for trial at the winter Assize for the wilful murder of his daughter. He was then handcuffed and taken by fly to the county gaol at Taunton.

Thornton visited him in gaol, and once more begged him to say what he had done with Anna; but Burgess would say nothing.

The search dragged on for a further two months, under the direction of Valentine Goold, with no progress being made. It was essential that Anna, or her body, be recovered if they were to hold Burgess, and the Dulverton magistrates became increasingly impatient, fearing that without more evidence, they would soon have to let Burgess go.

Then, at last, there was a breakthrough. Searchers were approached by a man, probably a sheep thief, who said he had information. He asked to see Thornton and offered to tell what he had seen if Thornton promised to overlook his nefarious activities. Thornton agreed.

The man said he had been out on the moor one night, and had seen Burgess making his way along the valley to the old Wheal Eliza iron mine, carrying what appeared to be a sack. He had watched him, and seen Burgess go in to the mine and come out again without his bundle.

Thornton took the information straight to Dulverton, and the magistrates immediately ordered the mine to be drained and searched.

Superintendent Jeffs engaged the services of Morris

Holward, a professional diver from the firm of Sadler and Company of Tooley Street, London, to inspect the mine and assess what would need to be done. Jeffs and Holward visited the mine together, and Holward estimated that a depth of at least 100 feet of water would have to be pumped out before it would be safe for a diver to go down.

A plan of the area was produced and shown to John Keene, a surveyor from Kingsbrompton, who testified it to be accurate, and Thomas Skews, a mining engineer from Molland, was paid £200 to carry out the task of draining the mine. The operation took several months and entailed the removal 220 feet of water.

On the 2nd December, Skews, together with his partner, John Moffat, was lowered into the shaft. At the bottom, they found a bag tied round with cord. Inside, was another bag and inside that, a mackintosh.

They took it to the surface and handed it to P C George Taylor who opened it and found inside, the body of a child. In his evidence at the trial, as reported by the Wells Journal on 25th December, Taylor said, '*it also contained a plaid shawl which was tied round the waist of the child, a black frock, a little jacket, a petticoat and shift which were on the body. The child had no shoes or boots on.*'

The shawl and mackintosh surrounding Anna's body when she was brought up from the mine, contained amounts of earth and broken pieces of rotten slate which, as Jeffs confirmed in his testimony at the trial later, matched the earth and slate he had found in the empty grave near Picked Stones.

The inner bag also contained two large stones, each weighing around 22 lbs.

The mineral content of the water in the mine had preserved the body, but once exposed to the air it would have begun to rapidly decompose, so it was placed in a box of water until it could be identified at the inquest. The box was nailed down and taken to the blacksmith's shop near the mine. The door was locked and Taylor took away the keys.

Taylor was then despatched to inform Superintendent Jeffs, who was already on his way. They met at Exford, and Jeffs sent Taylor on to Curry Rivel to inform the Coroner, before continuing on his way to the mine.

A post mortem was carried out on site by Dulverton surgeon, John Barrett Collins, assisted by Dr Sydenham and William Thomas Day, surgeon, of Williton.

The inquest was held on Saturday, 11th December, at the White Horse Inn at Exford, before W W Monckton, coroner of the country division. After the jury was sworn in, the court travelled to the Wheal Eliza mine to view the body which, according to the Tuesday edition of the Sherborne Mercury, *presented a horrid appearance.*

Collins said that, when he had removed the clothes,

he had found the body very much decomposed and sodden, having been in the water for some time. He said there was a skull fracture, caused by a heavy blunt instrument, but he did not think that would have been the cause of death, though it would eventually have been fatal; but it was more likely she had been suffocated.

Sarah Marley identified the body as Anna, saying she recognised her by her hair and her clothes. She confirmed that the boots Jeffs had found in Burgess's room in Swansea were the ones Anna had been wearing the day she left, and also said the mackintosh Anna was wrapped in was the same one she had often seen Burgess wearing.

Her statement was confirmed by William Cockram, the miner who shared the room with Burgess at Gallon House Cottage.

After hearing all the evidence, the jury delivered a verdict of wilful murder and the coroner issued a warrant of detainer to the governor of Taunton gaol where Burgess was being held.

Whether in a fit of remorse or in fear of hanging, Burgess tried, unsuccessfully, to commit suicide by cutting his throat with scissors.

He was committed to be tried at the Somerset Winter Assizes and, a few days later, stood trial before Mr Justice Byles. Mr Karslake and Mr King acted for the prosecution. Mr Rotten and Mr Murch, having been appointed by the court, acted for the defence.

The defence counsel attempted to bring a plea of insanity, possibly thinking of Burgess's brother who had died in the lunatic asylum; but he was unsuccessful, and Burgess was found guilty and sentenced to death.

On pronouncing sentence, the judge said: '...*The law of this land is that, "Who so sheddeth man's blood, by man shall his blood be shed." There is no hope of mercy for you in this world. The most advice which I can give is to resign yourself to the religious instruction which will be afforded to you, as the only way which you can expect to meet your fate with any degree of composure, resignation, or hope.*'

After his conviction, Burgess was visited several times by the prison Chaplain, Reverend Howse, and by Reverend Clarke, the curate of St Mary Magdelene church in Taunton.

He also asked to see Reverend Thornton who, as his parish priest, was obliged to hear his confession.

Burgess readily admitted to all three men that he had killed Anna merely so he could save the 2s 6d a week he'd had to pay for her keep, in order to spend it on drink instead. '*In any case,*' he'd said, '*she was in everyone's way and was better off dead*'.

An extract from his confession to Thornton was published in the Taunton Courier and Western Advertiser on Wednesday, 12th January 1859. '*I murdered my child for the purpose of saving 2s. 6d. per week, that I might be enabled thereby to indulge myself in more drink and to indulge drunkenness. I committed the awful deed. Do you, Sir, go back to Simonsbath, and tell the drunkards there to forsake drunkenness and strong drinks, or they may yet stand the condemned felon, I now stand.'*

He also confessed to burning down the farmhouse in which members of the Hayes household had died.

The evening before his execution, according to his gaolers, Burgess did not sleep, but got up between two and three o'clock to engage in prayer. He then took off the prison clothing and dressed in the clothes he had been wearing on his arrest. He ate breakfast and was visited by the prison governor, Mr Oakley, and by the Chaplain. At eight o'clock, he and some other prisoners were taken to the chapel where Divine Service was performed.

Reverend Clarke was of the opinion that Burgess was quite penitent, and he is said to have expressed a hope of *'salvation through the atoning blood of Christ'*. However, Burgess was denied Eucharist as the Chaplain thought him not fit to receive it.

As they left the chapel, the executioner, William Calcraft, put Burgess in pinions and, shortly after nine o'clock, led by Mr Sully the head turnkey and followed by the Chaplain reading the offices for the burial of the dead, they proceeded across the prison yard to the steps leading to the drop.

Burgess was hanged over the western entrance to Taunton county gaol, on 4th January 1859.

The following account of the execution was reported on 15th January 1859, in the Wells Journal:

Calcraft received the prisoner at the termination of the service, and having pinioned his arms, to which operation he submitted with a fortitude that had not been anticipated, the procession started to the scaffold.

A deep silence pervaded the multitude as the tolling of the chapel-bell gave signal that the funeral procession of the yet living culprit had started, and the boldest of their number held their breath as the gaol warder, followed by the chaplain, the criminal, and the executioner, mounted the scaffold.

Burgess walked firmly up, and was placed under the fatal beam. The chaplain concluded the reading of the burial-service. Calcraft performed his functions as the hangman. The preparations for carrying the sentence of the law into effect having been completed, the officials descended, leaving the culprit alone.

The bolt was almost immediately withdrawn, and, after a few throes of mortal agony, Burgess yielded up his life. In an hour afterwards the body was cut down and buried within the precincts of the gaol. The crowd dispersed almost as soon as the criminal was no more.

Anna Maria was buried in the churchyard of St Luke's church. Her grave was said to be unmarked but, behind the modern headstone can be seen what appears to be the remains of an older stone. Was this the original stone, perhaps erected by the villagers, or by Thornton, to mark the little girl's resting place?

A comforting thought; but, unfortunately, one with no evidence to support it.

The Grave of Anna Maria Burgess
showing the remains of an old headstone behind.
© 2023 Barry Hitchcox

Almost 150 years later, the location of the grave was identified by Stan Curtis of Simonsbath, and it was suggested the Exmoor Society might erect a memorial to mark the site.

A headstone was designed and made by stonemason, Peter Hayman of Taunton, with the inscription:

Anna Maria Burgess
Died in Tragic Circumstances
July 1858 Aged 6 years

The Grave of Anna Maria Burgess
© 2023 Barry Hitchcox

On 16th July 2000, following Sunday service, the congregation of St Luke, together with members of the Exmoor Society led by its Chairman, Michael Hawkins, gathered in the churchyard.

In a moving service, the Rector, Reverend Robin Ray, dedicated the memorial marking the final resting place of Anna Maria Burgess.

Stan and Millie Curtis with Michael Hawkins
at the dedication of the new headstone
© Steve Guscott
by kind permission of the Exmoor Society

THE CHILDREN

What happened to the children after the execution of their father?

Mary and John both went into service with James and Sarah Hayes at Southhill Farm.

On 28th March 1859, Mary married William Bale, a labourer, at St Andrew's Church in Withypool.

Mary and William had five children; Robert, Mary Anne, Jane, Alice and Ann. William Bale died in 1885 at the age of 56, and Mary moved to Dulverton, where she is listed on the census as being a widow of independent means. She died at Dulverton in 1917.

Jane and Charles went into service with John and Maria Hayes at Brinsworthy.

In 1869, Jane married William Passmore and moved to Warren House, Simonsbath. By 1891, they were living at Buttery Farm, North Molton.

Jane and William had six children; Richard, Sarah, Jane, Charley, Robert and Mary.

Jane died in 1911 aged 67 and William Passmore

died in 1916 aged 75.

Regarding the two boys, Charles and John, no further verifiable information has so far come to light.

THE PARISH OF EXMOOR

To appreciate how a situation like this could arise, it helps to understand what kind of place Exmoor was in the early to mid 19th century when the murder took place.

The old Forest of Exmoor was, like other ancient forests, a royal hunting ground; an area of land where strict laws were enforced to preserve game for the pleasure of the Crown.

It was first designated a royal hunting ground by the Saxons, but it was the Normans who began the process of removing trees and converting it into forest. Much of ancient Exmoor would have been densely wooded but deforestation was continued by subsequent kings until, by 1400, all woodland had been removed from the Devon forest to the west and from the western end of the Somerset forest to the east.

The Forest was administered, on behalf of the Crown, by a series of elected Wardens, who ensured the many complicated laws were strictly enforced. The slightest infringement could incur harsh and barbaric punishment such as the loss of ears or limbs, or the burning out of eyes.

The area was wild and lawless; and remained so until the mid nineteenth century.

The post of Warden was originally an hereditary one, passing from father to son. Later, it became an office which was leased from the Crown for a small sum, and which gave the Warden the right to extract payments from the population for such benefits as grazing their livestock.

In 1508, in addition to the wardenship of the Forest, the Forest itself was offered up for lease, eventually coming into the hands of the Dyke family and, in 1769, through marriage, to the Acland family.

In 1815, parliament passed an Act for *'investing in His Majesty certain parts of the Forest of Exmoor'*, and for enclosing the Forest.

The Forest was divided into allotments which were passed to those people who had formerly possessed rights. 3,000 acres were gifted to Thomas Acland of Holnicote, as compensation for losing the wardenship. The remainder, some 10,262 acres, became the King's personal property and was known as Simon's Bath Farm.

In 1818, the Crown decided to end the leasehold system for good, and the part of the Forest still in the ownership of the Crown was offered up for sale by public tender.

The highest bidder was John Knight, a Worcestershire Ironmaster, who bid £50,122.

By 1819 disafforestation of Exmoor was complete and the old forest laws no longer applied.

Knight now set about purchasing allotments from the other owners, and he soon owned around 20,000 acres. He introduced Cheviot sheep and began cultivating the moorland, removing even more of the remaining woodland. In 1841, his son, Frederick, took over management of the estate, building farms and roads, and beginning the construction of a stone wall round the perimeter of the estate; which he eventually inherited in 1850.

As part of the Inclosure Act, and thanks to some forward-thinking individual, a twelve acre plot of ground was reserved by the Crown for construction of a church; should Exmoor, at some future date, be in need of a place of worship.

Knight's agriculture and mining activities created opportunities for employment and, by 1845, the population of the Forest of Exmoor had grown sufficiently to warrant having its own church; the nearest one at the time being St Mary Magdelene at Exford, six miles away.

Eighteen residents presented a petition, asking for the church to be built.

In 1853, the plot of land set aside by the Crown was inspected and approved by the Commissioners, who also provided a grant of £1,815 towards the construction of the church and parsonage.

Designs were drawn up by architect Henry Clutton and, in 1855, Amos Hole of Kingsbrompton began building work. However, in his eagerness to win the contract, Hole had tendered too low and he eventually went bankrupt, owing some £500 to tradesmen. Another local builder, John How, was called in to complete the building.

On 18th October 1856, the church of St Luke was consecrated by the Bishop of Bath and Wells, the Rev Robert Eden, 3rd Baron Auckland.

St Luke's Church, Simonsbath
© 2023 Barry Hitchcox

Prior to 1856, the population of Exmoor had been too small to be given parish status. Indeed, until the early 19th century, the only house on the Forest was the one (now called Simonsbath House) built by the first warden, James Boevey. It had stood in isolation for 150 years. But by 1856, as a result of the influx of labour, the population was deemed large enough to be granted parish status, and the Parish of Exmoor was created out of the old Royal Forest.

The first vicar of the newly established Exmoor parish was the Reverend William Henry Thornton.

Exmoor was, and is, the largest, most sparsely populated, parish on Exmoor; thirty-two square miles of mainly farmland and open moorland.

The two centres of population are the village of Simonsbath and the hamlet of Sandyway. Even today, the population numbers less than one hundred and fifty people.

The nearest town was North Molton, eleven miles away, and the nearest police station was twenty-four miles away at Wiveliscombe. In an area as isolated and under-populated as this, it would have been all too easy for William Burgess to kill and dispose of his daughter, then to disappear and escape to Wales.

THE WHEAL ELIZA MINE

The Wheal Eliza mine (originally called Wheal Maria) is the site of the first recorded mining in the Royal Forest of Exmoor; although the first activity on the site is thought to have been around 1552.

The word 'wheal' derives from the Cornish word 'huel' meaning 'working'.

Situated on the river Barle, about a mile downstream from Simonsbath, Wheal Eliza was one of the projects undertaken by the Knight family in the early 19th century.

The mine consisted of two main shafts, excavated to about 300 feet, which were pumped out by machinery powered by a waterwheel, driven by two leats, installed in 1847. On the south side of the river were the two leats, a wheel pit and the tail race. On the north side of the river were the shafts and spoil heaps.

Overlooking the mine, were an accounts house, the

buildings for supporting crafts such as blacksmiths and carpenters, and a two-room cottage in which five or more miners were housed.

A group of South Molton businessmen operated it as a copper mine from 1845 to 1854. Although evidence was found of copper ore, it was deemed insufficient to make the mine viable, so none was ever extracted and the mine was abandoned.

Two years later, in 1856, The Barrow Haematite Company re-opened Wheal Eliza; this time as an iron mine. However, no iron was found and the mine closed in1857. The workings were abandoned and allowed to flood.

The derelict Wheal Eliza Mine
by kind permission of The Exmoor Society

All that now remains of the Wheal Eliza mine is the pit for the water wheel, and parts of the shaft head with its rising main and pump rod. On the north side of the river, spoil heaps and some platforms and footings for the mine buildings remain. On the south side, the two leats can still be seen, and the tail race running up the valley.

After the closure of the mine, the cottage was inhabited by shepherds. The last occupants were shepherd William Little and his family, who lived there until 1952. When they left, the buildings were abandoned and left to slowly decay.

Wheal Eliza Cottages c 1950
by kind permission of the Exmoor Society

Wheal Eliza Cottages c 1970
by kind permission of the Exmoor Society

The following drawing, copied from an old photograph, possibly taken in the early 20th century, looking WNW from the south side of the River Barle, shows the site as virtually derelict except for the cottage and outbuildings. The track to Simonsbath curves away NW over the hill to the right of Flexbarrow.

The overshot waterwheel was mounted in the hillside on the extreme left foreground of the picture, and was supplied by a leat running along the hill beyond. A driveshaft carried power from the wheel across the river to the pump above the mineshaft.

The main mineshaft was to the far right of the picture with a main spoil heap to its left and possibly another to its right.

REVEREND THORNTON

First Vicar of the Parish of Exmoor

The Reverend William Henry Thornton (1830-1916) was the first vicar of the parish of Exmoor.

He was born in Clapham Common, London, in 1830, the youngest of twelve children born to John Thornton (1783-1861) and his wife Elizabeth, nee Parry (1787-1863). His father was Deputy Chairman of the Board of Inland Revenue, and Commissioner of Stamps and Taxes, employed in the tax department at Somerset House.

At the age of seventeen, while at Rugby school, Thornton became seriously ill with cholera; possibly as a result of eating contaminated un-ripe fruit.

He was sent to stay with a friend in the small hamlet of Allerford, near Porlock, to recover and convalesce and, while there, he enjoyed the country sports of hunting, shooting and fishing. He loved riding, and throughout his life he thought nothing of riding vast distances.

He grew to love Porlock, which he called his 'happy valley', and while there he met Sir Thomas Acland, the 11th baronet, who allowed him to wander around the extensive lands of the Holnicote Estate.

Thornton was a regular visitor to Glenthorne at Countisbury, where he met and became friends with the Knight family of Simonsbath; in particular Frederick Knight. He also made the acquaintance of John 'Jack' Russell, the sporting parson from Swimbridge in Devon, famed for his breed of Jack Russell terriers.

Recovered from his illness, in 1849, Thornton went up to Trinity College Cambridge where, in 1853, he gained a BA. He was later awarded an MA in 1859. At the same time, he also studied for the voluntary theological examination, which he passed in October 1853. In December of that year, he was ordained at Exeter Cathedral and was offered, and accepted, the curacy of Lynton and Countisbury in Devon.

In Countisbury, he established a school, where he himself taught, but he stayed for only two years before resigning the curacy in order to accept the post, offered to him by his friend Frederick Knight, of vicar of the newly created parish of Exmoor.

In 1856, he took over the living at the newly built

vicarage and church of St Luke in Simonsbath. It was a large and isolated parish, and a later obituary mentions that he *'regularly embarked on a fifty mile ride or a twenty or thirty mile walk across the moors'*.

In 1857, he married Grace Anne Furnival (1826-1916) daughter of the Reverend James Furnival. Grace bore him eight children, two of which died in infancy. Their first-born child was buried in St Luke's churchyard in 1858, the same year that Thornton became involved with William Burgess and the murder of Anna Maria at the Wheal Eliza mine.

After the loss of the child, and with the doctor so far away (it was eleven miles to the nearest town, North Molton) Grace felt the parish was too remote. She no longer felt safe and could not settle. So, in 1860, they moved to Dunsford in Devon; but they both missed the moorland air and, in 1866, they moved once again to take up the living at North Bovey on Dartmoor.

In 1871, Thornton was elected Rural Dean of the Deanery of Moretonhampstead, an office he held for eight years.

He became well-known for his many articles and papers, which he contributed to literary, historical and scientific journals. He also wrote *Reminiscences of a West Country Clergyman*, which was published in two volumes in 1897 and 1899.

They remained at North Bovey for fifty years. Thornton died on the 31st of March 1916, a few months before Grace, who died in December. They are buried, side by side, in Bovey churchyard.

Reverend William Henry Thornton
the first vicar of the parish of Exmoor

AFTERTHOUGHTS

Although contemporary accounts of William Burgess and the murder of Anna Maria are, on the whole, in agreement as to the facts, more recent re-tellings of the story have proved less accurate; possibly through a lack of serious research or, more likely, due to a desire to dramatise and romanticise the story.

One of the most common inconsistencies is that William and Jane Burgess had three children, Tom, Emma and Anna. There were many families on Exmoor, and especially in the Porlock area, called Burgess; and one of those families did indeed have children called Tom, Emma and Anna.

In the 19th century, people rarely moved far from their home village. Before the days of public transport, travel for most villagers meant walking or, if they could afford it, taking the carrier's cart. Consequently, marriages tended to be between members of the same village and, as a result, families developed many branches, and the same surnames came to dominate.

Christian names also tended to be repeated, as they were handed down from father to son and mother to daughter. In William Burgess's case, his older brother, John, was named after their father, and his sister, Betty, was named after their mother. So it is no wonder there were several men called William Burgess in Porlock.

So the mistake is an easy one to make. But genealogical research clearly shows that William Burgess and Jane Shapland had five children; Mary, Jane, John, Charles and Hannah Maria.

Some accounts suggest the reason for Burgess wanting to be rid of Anna is that, after Jane's death, he wished to remarry, but the woman refused to take Anna. In all the contemporary accounts, and the testimonies at the various hearings, there is no mention at all of any such plans, or of any such woman.

The reason most commonly given, and which is born out by all the evidence, is simply that Burgess was an alcoholic whose life was completely ruled by his addiction and, faced with a choice between paying for his daughter's keep and feeding his habit, the drink won.

There are confused accounts about where, precisely, in Porlock, Burgess was intending (or said he was intending) to take Anna. In some accounts, he was taking Anna to stay with his mother at Porlock. In others, he was taking her to his sister at Porlock Weir. Although they seem to contradict each other, all accounts are correct. There are three parts to the village of Porlock; the main village; the harbour of Porlock Weir, a mile away on the coast; and West Porlock part way between the two. In giving evidence at Burgess's trial, John Moore, who was married to Burgess's sister Betty, stated that they lived in West Porlock and that his mother-in-law, who was ill and bedridden, lived with them.

It has already been mentioned that, in contemporary accounts, Anna is called Hannah. Quite why she has come to be known as Anna is uncertain. It could possibly originate from a misreading of her name in the digitised documents which are, in many cases, almost indecipherable. Interestingly, though, she is referred to as Anna in the baptism register. Maybe, the two were interchangeable.

For the same reason, transcripts of the court hearings, and of the newspaper reports, occasionally disagree as to a person's name. For instance, Mary Farley is sometimes referred to as Mary Fraley; the mining engineer, Thomas Skews, as Thomas Hughes; William Day, the surgeon, as William Gaye; the defence lawyer Rotten as Hotton; and Chief Constable Goold as Gould or Good. Where this has happened, I have used the most commonly used (though not necessarily correct) version.

ONE FINAL THOUGHT

The case against William Burgess is pretty damning; but, was he really as evil as he appears to be?

After all, he did make the effort to find homes for his children, when he could quite easily have deserted them. There was nothing preventing him from disappearing and leaving them to fend for themselves.

Surprisingly, there are several indications that perhaps he wasn't wholly bad. His attempt to commit suicide by cutting his throat with the scissors, could just have been an attempt to avoid the horror of hanging. On the other hand, perhaps it was in genuine remorse for what he had done.

It is certainly born out by testimony at the trial, when Jeffs told the court that, when he had arrested him at Swansea, Burgess had said to him: '*I did it and shall never be happy any more ... I would have saved you the trouble to come and fetch me by making away with myself. I ought to have done so before.'*

The reporter from the Wells Journal, reporting on the trial on 25 December 1858, noted that: '*He hung his head on the front of the dock and appeared to be overcome with emotion.*'

The Bridgewater Mercury reported that, '*His manner in court, with the exception of the two occasions when he interrupted the witnesses, was subdued and respectful, and the attention he paid to the witnesses was very remarkable.*'.

Testimony given at the trial by witnesses, also suggests another side to him.

Evidence of John Collins surgeon: '*He was kind to his children as far as I know.*'

Evidence of Mrs Marley: '*I never saw the prisoner behave otherwise than kindly towards his child while he lived with me ... he was generally a cheerful man.*'

Evidence of William Cockram miner: '*I never saw any bad conduct of his towards the child. He never complained to me he was paying too much for the child.*'

Evidence of William Smith, shoemaker, of North Molton: '*I know the prisoner. On the 30th of May he gave me a nice order for a pair of boots for his little girl.*'

Given its wild and lawless state, life on Exmoor at that time must have been incredibly hard, and it would have been very easy for a young William to become drawn into bad company. There is no doubt he was an alcoholic and, without the steadying hand of his wife, Jane, he soon became a slave to his addiction.

Appalling and unforgivable though his crime was, might there have been a better person buried somewhere beneath the drunken murderer he became?

Perhaps.

BIBLIOGRAPHY

Ancestry.com. https://www.ancestry.com/

Archive, The British Newspaper. " Execution at Taunton. Wells Journal - Saturday 15 January 1859 ." British Newspaper Archive, 15 Jan. 1859, https://www.britishnewspaperarchive.co.uk/viewer/bl/0000308/18590115/038/0005?browse+=+false.

Archive, The British Newspaper. "Execution of William Burgess for the Murder of His Child. Taunton Courier, and Western Advertiser - Wednesday 12 January 1859 ." Register | British Newspaper Archive, https://www.britishnewspaperarchive.co.uk/viewer/bl/0000348/18590112/001/0002?browse+=+false.

Archive, The British Newspaper. "The Exmoor Forest Murder. Sherborne Mercury - Tuesday 14 December 1858 ." Register

| British Newspaper Archive, https://www.britishnewspaperarchive.co.uk/viewer/bl/0000411/18581214/024/0006?browse+=+false.

Archive, The British Newspaper. “The Exmoor Murder. Wells Journal - Saturday 25 December 1858 .” Register | British Newspaper Archive, https://www.britishnewspaperarchive.co.uk/viewer/bl/0000308/18581225/053/0008?browse+=+false.

Archive, The British Newspaper. “The Exmoor Murder. Bridgwater Mercury - Wednesday 12 January 1859 .” Register | British Newspaper Archive, https://www.britishnewspaperarchive.co.uk/viewer/bl/0002058/18590112/109/0008?browse+=+false.

“Executedtoday.com.” ExecutedToday.com " 1859: William Burgess, http://www.executedtoday.com/2016/01/07/1859-william-burgess/.

British Newspaper Archive. https://www.britishnewspaperarchive.co.uk/

Exmoor Review. 2001. Vol 42. page 13. "Crying the Moor." "Memorial for Anna".

Exmoor National Park HER (ENPHER). “Exmoor National Park Authority/ Wheal Eliza Mine (Monument).” MSO6802 - Wheal Eliza Mine - The Historic Environment Record for Exmoor National Park, 11 Oct. 2022, https://www.exmoorher.co.uk/Monument/MSO6802.

FamilySearch.org. https://www.familysearch.org/en/

Genealogy Online. https://www.genealogieonline.nl/en/

Kilda, St. “Wheal Eliza and the Murder of Anna Maria Burgess.” Wheal Eliza and the Murder of Anna Maria Burgess, 1 Jan. 1970, http://offthebeatentrackinsomerset.blogspot.com/2016/08/wheal-eliza-and-murder-of-anna-maria.html.

Linham, Laura. “Dark Somerset: The Man Who Killed His Daughter for Beer Money.” SomersetLive, 13 Apr. 2018, https://www.somersetlive.co.uk/news/somerset-news/dark-somerset-man-who-killed-1440112.

Wikipedia, Wikipedia. “Wheal Eliza Mine.” Wikipedia, Wikimedia Foundation, 20 Apr. 2022, https://en.wikipedia.org/wiki/Wheal_Eliza_Mine.

Wikiwand. "William Henry Thornton." Wikiwand. William Henry Thornton., https://www.wikiwand.com/simple/The_Reverend_William_Thornton_(1830-1916).

ABOUT THE AUTHOR

Gail Crane

Gail Crane spent most of her life in Oxfordshire before moving to Exmoor on retirement. She has always had a fascination for history, and soon became engrossed with the history and legends of Exmoor and its people.

She started writing in her twenties, producing articles and short stories for magazines, stories for children's comics, and numerous verses for greetings cards, until the demands of family, a full time job, and setting up and running a business, meant writing took a back seat, and it wasn't until she retired, that she began writing seriously again.

She has published two romance novels, inspired by the moors and coast of Exmoor, and her short stories have been published in magazines, and as collections in books. Her growing interest in the history of Exmoor, inspired her first non-fiction work, The Murder of Anna Maria, the true story of notorious Exmoor murderer, William Burgess.

This was followed by "Stained Glass in Exmoor Churches", an illustrated exploration of the stories behind the images in the windows.

In 2014 she successfully completed a BA (Hons) degree with Open University, studying creative writing, and is a member of the Alliance of Independent Authors.

BOOKS BY THIS AUTHOR

Flynn's Folly

An Exmoor Romance Novel.

When wealthy hotelier, Max Corrigan, claims part ownership of The Folly, Jessica Flynn is not about to give in without a fight. Even if he is drop-dead gorgeous.

Following the death of her father, Jessica returns to The Folly, her home on Exmoor, to find the house neglected and a once thriving business on the verge of collapse. So why has Max Corrigan invested so much money in it? And who exactly is he?

Corrigan wants his investment repaid and until then he expects a say in the running of the business but Jessica has no intention of letting a stranger take over and determines to repay the debt; and to do that she needs help. Who can she turn to?

As she struggles to find a solution, she is no longer sure who she can trust, and realises she is in danger of losing everything, including her heart.

Master Of Hanging Cross

An Exmoor Romance Novel.

Kate Mckenzie is off men and finished with love.

The last thing Ethan Cade wants is to get involved with another woman. He's been caught once and has no intention of repeating the experience.

Disillusioned with her work and reeling from a broken relationship, Kate leaves London for Hanging Cross, an isolated estate on Exmoor overlooking the sea, to begin a new job as personal assistant to a famous novelist.

From the moment he sees her, Ethan is determined Kate will have to go, but Kate has found her dream job and is equally determined to stay, despite Ethan's hostility. Her position becomes even more uncomfortable when fate brings them into a close working relationship.

As the secrets of Hanging Cross gradually unfold, and her own past eventually catches up with her, Kate must act, or leave Hanging Cross for good.

Stained Glass In Exmoor Churches

NON FICTION

Across Exmoor, ancient churches keep watch over moor and village. Their windows, the stone embrasures, tracery and mullions, are often described in great detail, but of the beautiful stained glass within, there is rarely a mention.

In each overlooked window, filled with names and images from the past, there is a hidden story waiting to be told. Who were these people? What did they do? Why are they remembered here?

This beautifully illustrated book attempts to answer some of these questions, and reveal the intriguing history behind the stained glass windows in Exmoor churches.

Printed in Dunstable, United Kingdom

74897702R00037